The Snowman

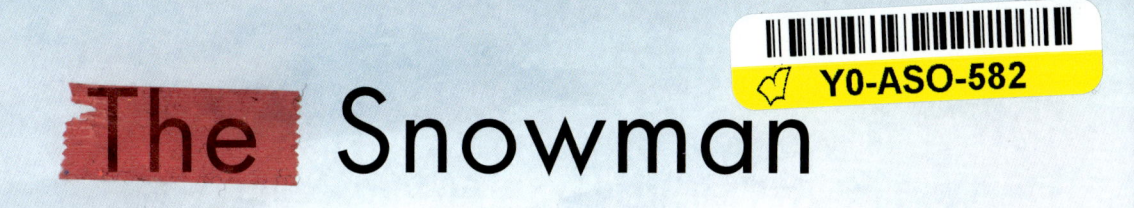

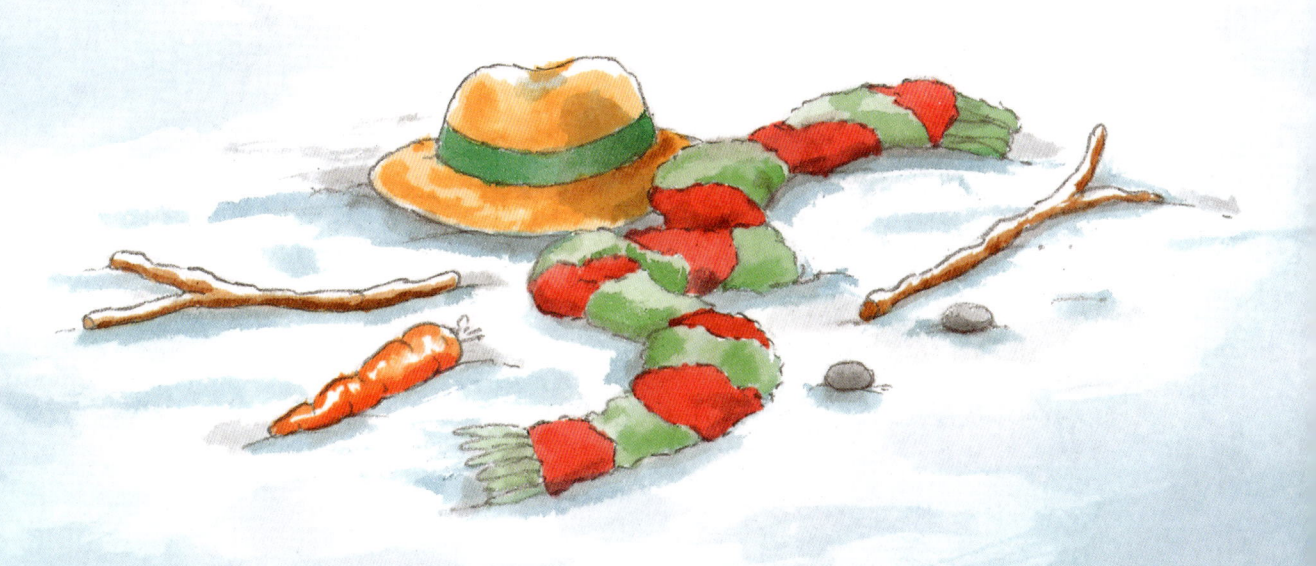

Written by Carol Krueger
Illustrated by Madeline Beasley

We made a snowman.

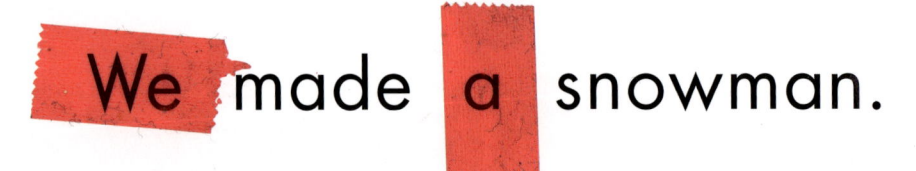

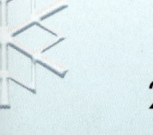

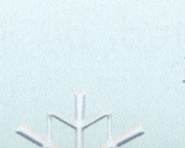

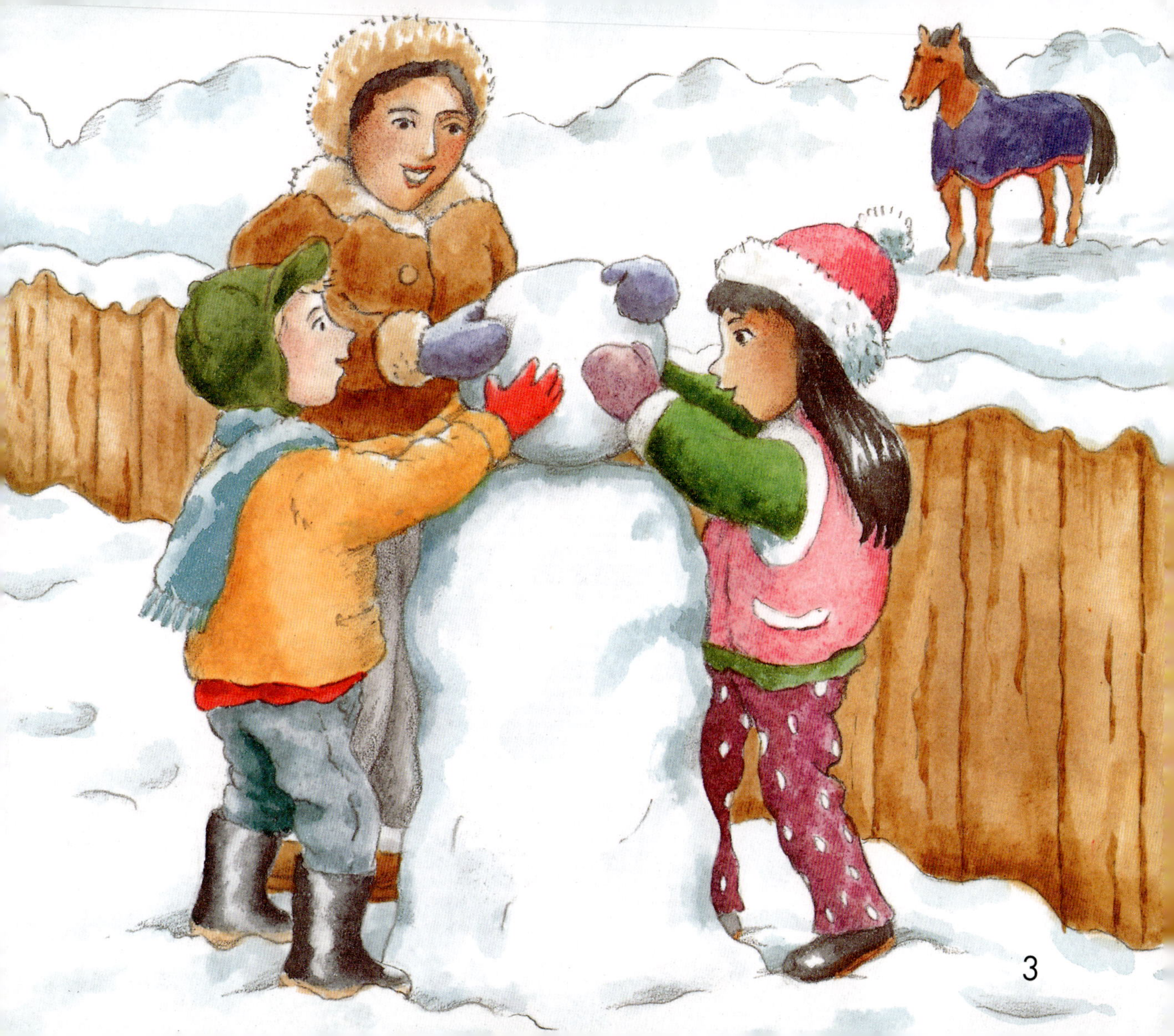

We gave him arms.

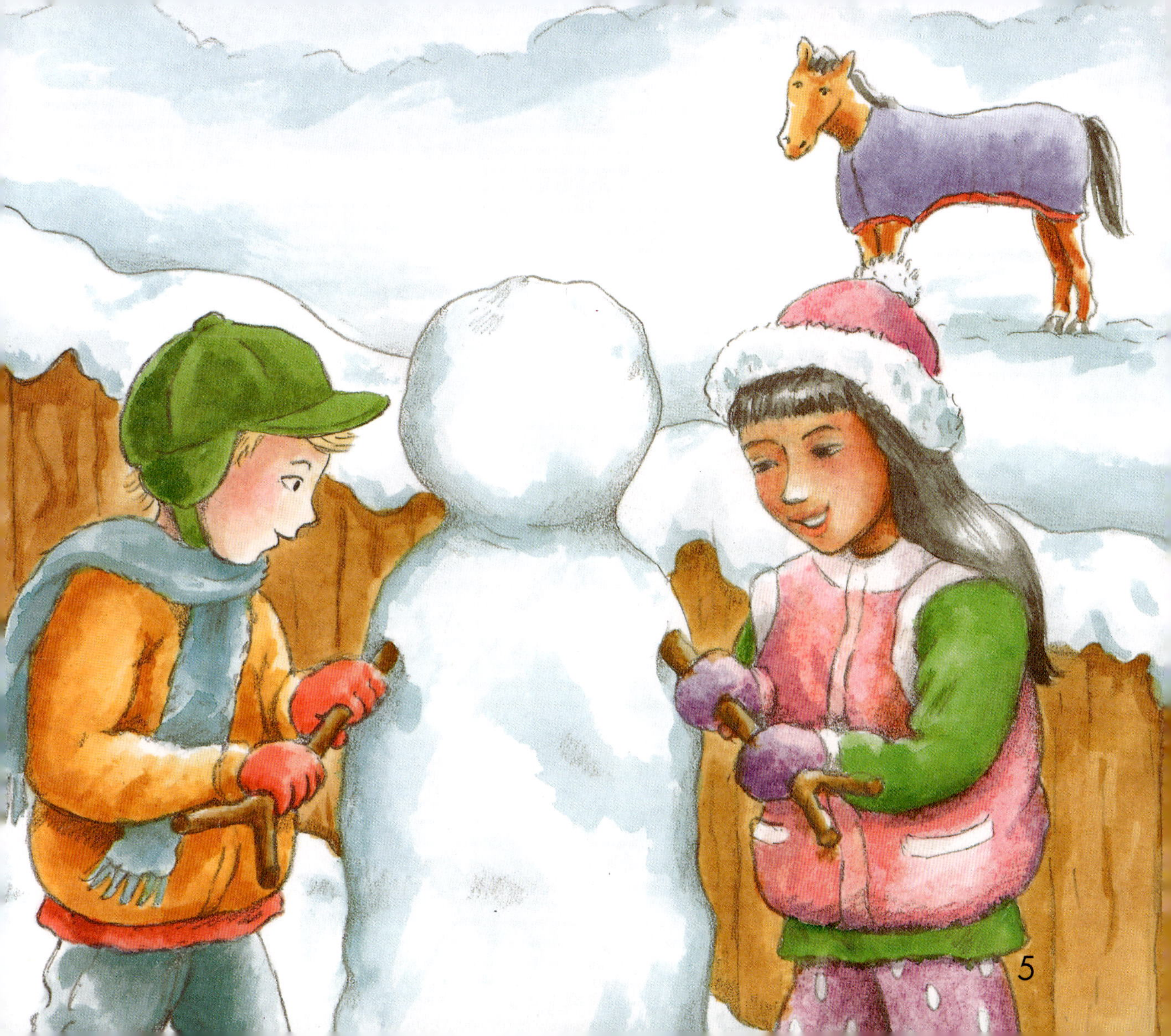

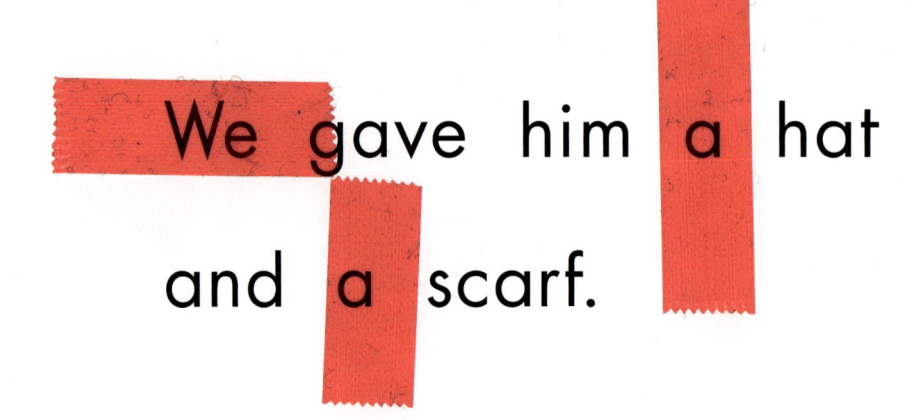

We gave him a hat
and a scarf.

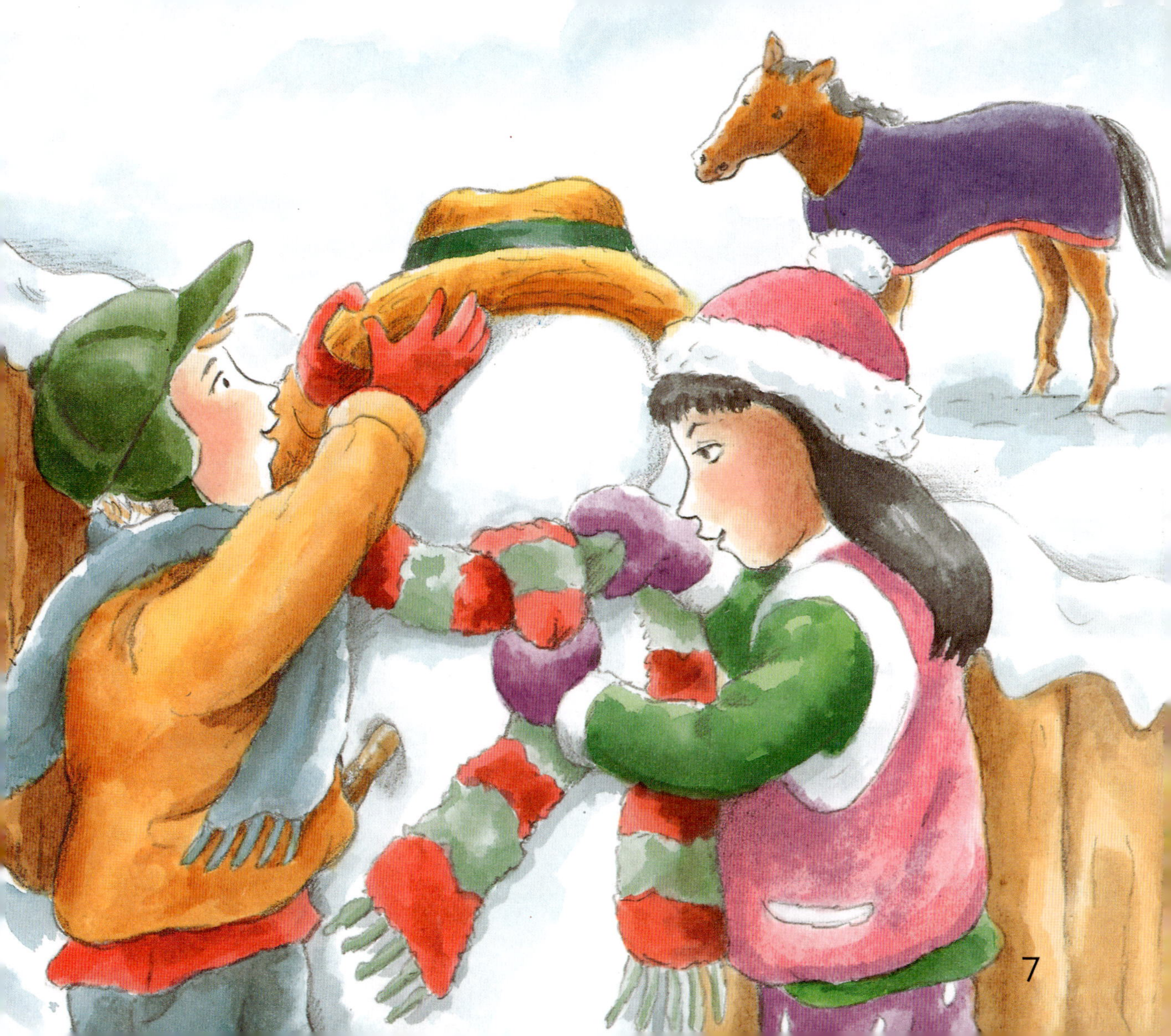

We gave him eyes
and a mouth.

9

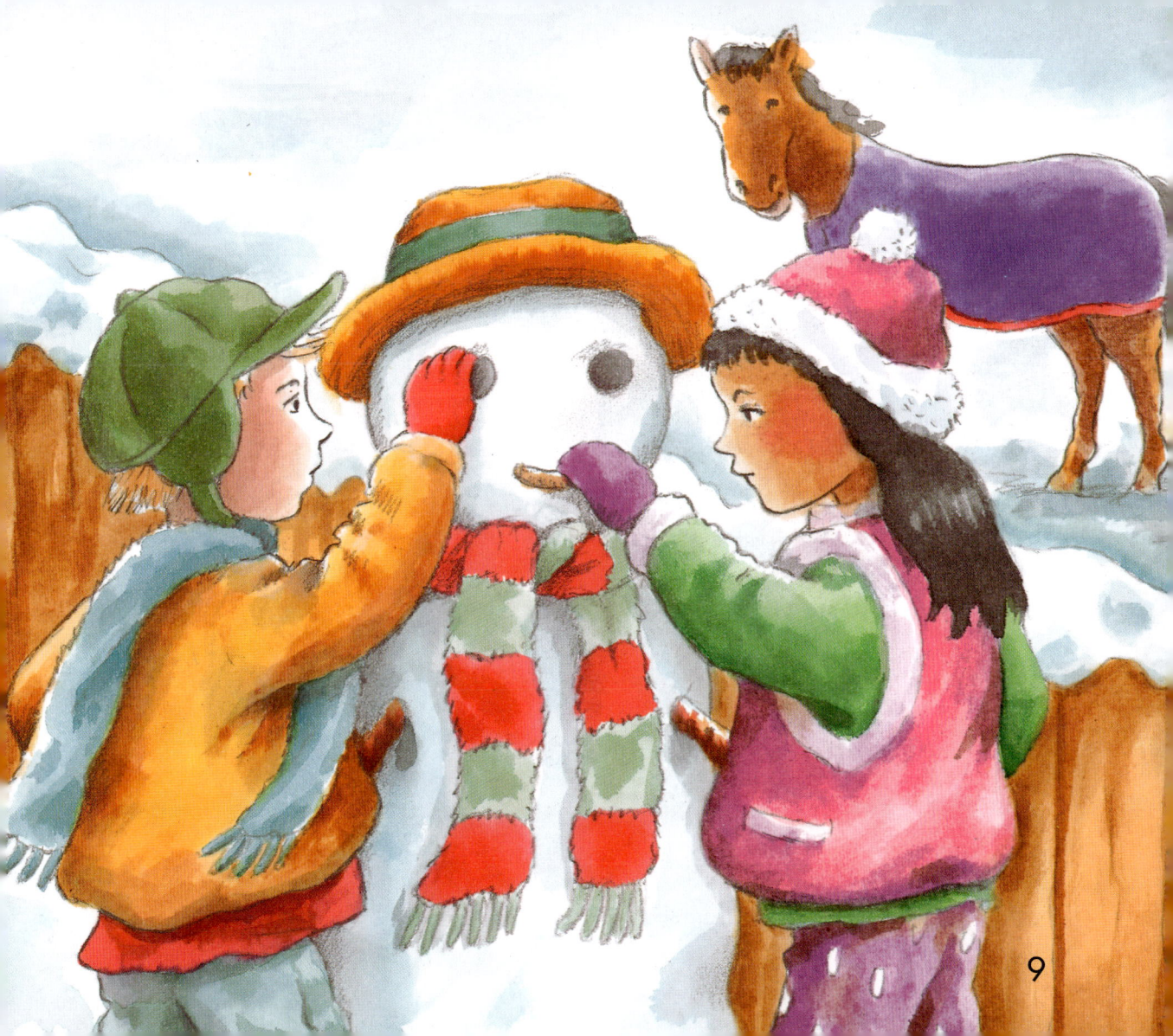

We gave him a nose...

11

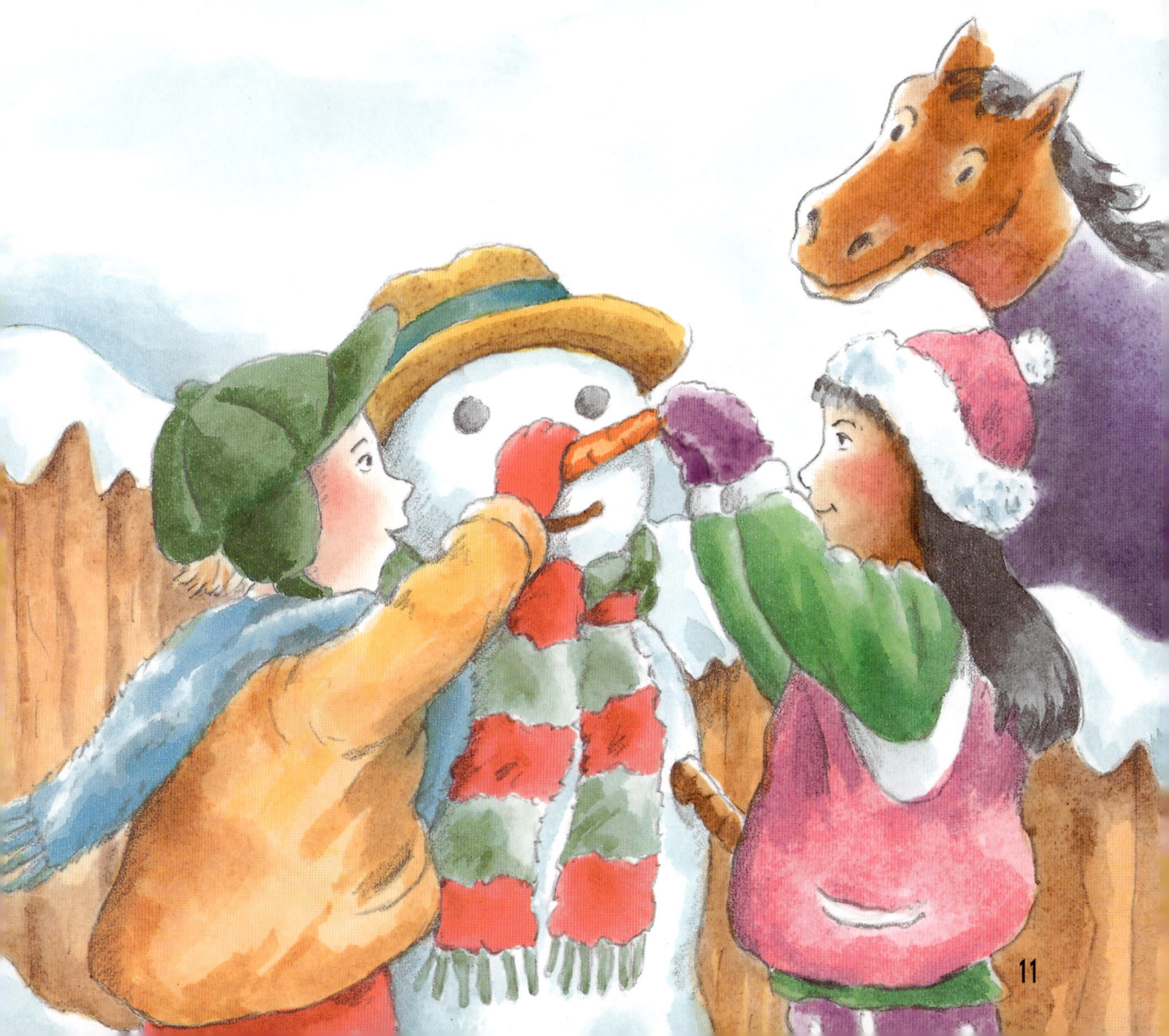

but the horse ate it!

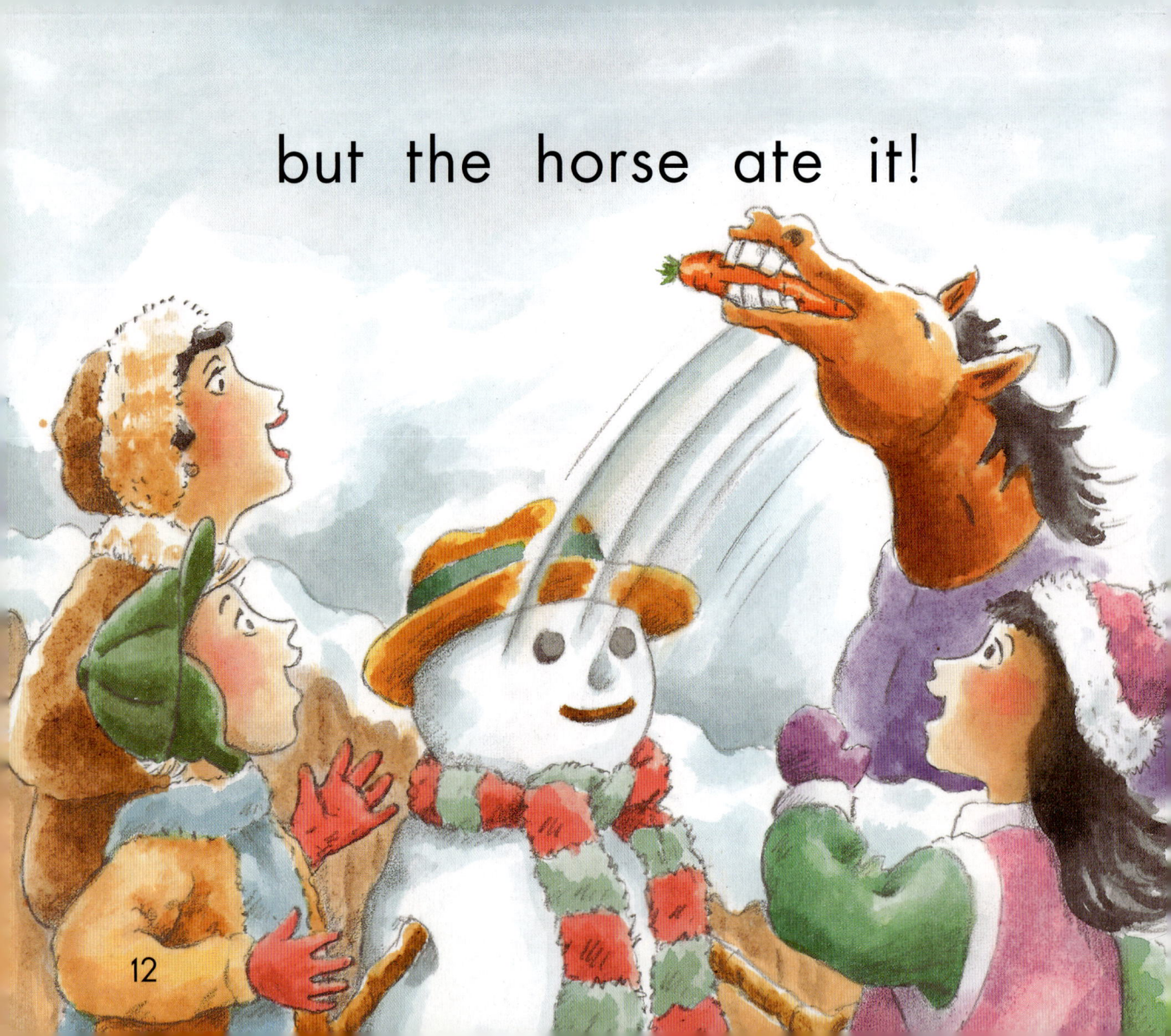